*With grateful thanks to all those who faithfully pray for the work of MAF and our teams around the developing world.*

Published by Mission Aviation Fellowship UK
Castle Hill Avenue
Folkestone
Kent
CT20 2TN
UK

*Telephone*: +44(0)1303 850950
*Email*: supporter.relations@maf-uk.org
*Website*: www.maf-uk.org

Mission Aviation Fellowship UK is part of Mission Aviation Fellowship International.

Copyright © 2013 Mission Aviation Fellowship

Mission Aviation Fellowship asserts the moral right to be identified as the author of this work.

A catalogue record for this book is available from the British Library.

ISBN 978-0-9927160-1-1

Further copies can be obtained directly from MAF UK

Typeset in the United Kingdom by documen, www.documen.co.uk
Printed in the United Kingdom
Print Production by Roperpenberthy Publishing Limited

# CONTENTS

# INTRODUCTION

In many countries of the developing world MAF is bringing help, hope and healing to people living in isolation.

Unseen is the prayer, love and practical support of so many 'ground crew'. I believe that because of their prayers for MAF, accidents have been avoided, people have been protected and doors which were shut have been opened.

When the concept of MAF was considered in 1945, Murray Kendon wrote:

'Gather into a prayer fellowship as many as possible who are vitally interested in the hastening of world evangelisation by the use of the aeroplane.'

Today we say that prayer is the foundation of the work of MAF. Again and again we have seen the mighty hand of God intervene in the daily work of MAF with miracles of favour, blessing, provision and protection.

Someone once asked me, 'How can you measure prayer?' The reply came: 'When we see the miraculous in our everyday lives'.

So often we see prayers answered in MAF, but how often will we remember to thank the Lord and give Him the glory? We see the miraculous in our everyday lives – but do we take it for granted?

Philippians 4:6 says: *'Do not worry. Learn to pray about everything. Give thanks to God as you ask Him for what you need.'*

We are so very thankful for the prayers and faithful support of the many people who make our ministry possible.

I have had the privilege of being part of many prayer meetings, and have been encouraged through the devotions, verses and prayers of the support team in the UK and also from our overseas staff who are on the MAF 'frontline'.

We have compiled some of these devotions from MAF personnel around the world. I trust they will encourage you and help you to feel connected and in fellowship with our team and with the Lord Jesus Christ.

Thank you for your support – and your continuing prayers!

The Lord bless you.

*Ruth Whitaker*
*Chief Executive, MAF UK*

# The Good Gardener

*'I am the true vine, and My Father is the vinedresser.'*

(John 15:1)

I was recently re-reading John 15:1 about the vine, the branches and the gardener. Jesus is the vine, you and I are the branches – but the gardener is our Father God.

I have read this many times before – no doubt you have too – but Scripture always speaks again. These thoughts are just a reminder.

All of us have experienced times when we have had to face 'pruning'. Such times may have been deep and painful. I know that has been true in my own life. But these seasons have been needed. Some of my greatest and most lasting growth has resulted from going through such periods.

I was thinking about this and sitting looking out on my garden. It's only small, but is quite beautiful. When I say that it is 'my' garden, I really should be saying it was my late wife's garden. I helped in setting it up but she did all the planting. And she loved gardening. She knew when and where to plant things. She knew when they needed transplanting. She knew what kind of soil they needed. She watched that weeds didn't choke them.

And she knew when to prune and by how much. She was a good gardener. But my heavenly Father is not only a good gardener, He is the perfect gardener. The One who knows the absolute best for me.

Jesus says that the Father *'cuts off every branch that does not bear fruit, while every branch that does bear fruit He prunes so that it will be even more fruitful'* (John 15:2).

Some aspects of my life may be hampering its full growth. God wants my life to be more and more beautiful and fruitful. Pruning is always about enhancing the beauty and health of the plant. And the most prolific and beautiful plants, *e.g.* rhododendrons, often need the most pruning or they can choke the life of those growing around them!

We can thank God for the fruit He has privileged us to bear. But where do we need to bear more fruit? What is it that may still need pruning? I am praying for understanding and willingness as to what the 'Good Gardener', my loving heavenly Father, wants to do in my life.

Pruning needs to be a regular thing. It's not a 'one off' matter. At the right season, right time and in the right amount, it is essential for the branches' growth, health and beauty. And so it is with us.

*Stuart King*
*Co-founder and President Emeritus, MAF International*

# The Clay, the Potter and the Wheel

*'Go down to the shop where clay pots and jars are made and I will talk to you there.'*

(Jeremiah 18:2)

Some years ago, on holiday in Wales, our family visited a local pottery. Not only could you watch the craft in action, you were invited to make your own pottery mug under the expert direction of a real, live potter, in front of a real, live audience.

For some reason, I stuck my hand up, went to the front, was duly encased in a large apron, and put in front of a small potter's wheel. Clay was centred on the wheel, the motor started and the lesson began. It was an education.

Anybody who thinks that clay is an inert material has never tried working with it! As a material it is stubborn, wilful, independent and non-co-operative. To the people who – like me – had queued up to watch, it was highly entertaining. To me, it was a battle. The clay would not stay still. It didn't want to be moulded and had no intention of passively submitting to my intentions for it.

Strange really – when the local artist does it, the clay seems to bend, become compliant, working with the potter in the thrilling process of discovering just what ornamental or useful object it might become. One minute it's a shapeless lump of brown material, the next it's a living, growing thing, taking shape within the skilful hands of an artist, and becoming an elegant jug or a sturdy bowl.

Of course they use a completely different kind of clay to what I was given to work with. There's no other explanation! Theirs worked with them; mine fought back. They had clay with the right motivation, clay that wanted to become something beautiful. I had clay with attitude. It was a battle of wills.

I was determined to win, but the clay had strategies I had never heard of. As the visitors watched and laughed, it all slipped away from me. The clay became irregular, deformed, and bits of it left the wheel. The instructor did her best – but at the end of the demonstration there was no question who had won.

I got a badge, the visitors got a lesson, my family got a lot of fun at my expense and what came home with me was a permanent reminder of how not to make something. It was neither decorative nor useful, just a reminder of my complete lack of skill as a potter.

But that was the point. The secret was never in the clay. It was always in the hands of the potter. The only thing the clay contributes is itself. It has to be there, on the wheel. It has to stay inside the potter's hands long enough for the potter's skill to create what the potter's vision has seen. The clay does nothing. The potter does it all.

And God says: 'Stay on the wheel, let me finish what I have started. You can do nothing, I can do anything.' What makes the difference between the life that is shabby and ordinary, and the life that shines with God's character and behaviour is that one lump of clay remaining on the wheel long enough for the potter to finish the job.

We bring nothing to the splendid thing God is creating. We are what we are... clay. God brings everything to it. He has the wisdom. He has the knowledge. He has the patience and He has the skill. His hands work the miracle and under them we become what we are not. Doesn't the Bible say, *'He takes the things that are not'* (1 Corinthians 1:28)?

The finished product on the shelves of the pottery draws admiring glances. Some are truly inspired. But no one says, 'What wonderful clay that is'. As we stand and marvel at the elegance, the beauty of shape and symmetry, all we say is, 'How did they do that with just a lump of clay?' And there lies the reason for both humility and hope.

Humility, because whatever truly good thing comes out of a life, it was put there by God. If you see God in any part of my life and character, look closely and you will see the Potter's fingerprints all over it. And hope, because whatever I am right now – formless, shapeless, useless; without place, purpose or value – who knows what I will become if I only stay on the wheel and let the Potter keep working?

My final value cannot be measured by what I am now. It can only be measured by the limitless skill and expertise, the patience and resourcefulness of the Potter.

I may well be spoilt. To others, even beyond salvage. How often have I been written off? I am a failure at what I am. But the Potter sits down, patiently, skilfully and persistently reworking the clay that no one else can see any future for.

And as He works, another miracle is born between His fingers. I am made into something else. I can no longer be what I might have been. But I do not have to remain what I am. I can be whatever He wants me to be!

There is hope enough in that for every piece of clay. So long as He is the Potter. And so long as we stay on the wheel.

*Shared by Rachel Phipps*
*(written by her father, Brian Thompson)*
*Human Resources Manager, MAF UK*

# Holy Ground

*"Do not come any closer," God said. "Take off your sandals, for the place where you are standing is holy ground."'*

(Exodus 3:5)

I'm not an outwardly passionate person, particularly when it comes to worship. I don't dance in the aisles at church and – let's be honest – I don't even raise my hands in worship, but it was all different one morning.

I was in hospital with an undiagnosed and possibly life-threatening condition which had blocked my bowel. For five days I had been going downhill and was in a pitiable state, with fluids being drained out through my nose and elsewhere, and others coming in through my arm with morphine to dull my pain – feeling miserable. I had lost all my energy, couldn't concentrate and struggled to answer the nurses' simplest questions and, as I had become physically weaker, my emotional strength had ebbed away too. The doctors had decided they would open me up to find out what was going on and I knew that frequently such blockages come from a cancerous tumour. Morbid thoughts about leaving my wife Angela and our boys filled my mind.

So there I was in the quiet of the 'men's clinical' ward at 5am on an overcast and drizzly English morning, feeling very low. Not only was I thinking about the consequences of dying but I was recalling poor decisions I had made, things I had failed to do, my lack of spiritual discipline and the many ways I must be a disappointment to God. Eventually I came to a point of previously unknown vulnerability and uncertainty and feebly cried out to God, 'Lord, am I alright with you?' Instantly a powerful burning sensation roared up from my feet and seemed to explode in my head, filling me with an indescribable sense of acceptance and overwhelming love – it was wonderful.

For the next 20 minutes or so, flat on my back in that men's ward, I lay with tears of joy streaming down my face and tube-pierced arms fully raised, just praising God, consumed by His presence, love and acceptance – utterly at peace. Despite the medical paraphernalia – it was holy ground.

May we all be aware of the holiness of every moment of each day as we worship and serve our loving God, present with us.

*Bill Harding*
*International Development Director*

# Praying into the Unknown?

The Bible has a lot to say about prayer but there is much we do not fully understand.

We do not understand the mystery of why God chooses to have us play our part in His plan of salvation through our prayers, but we do know that *'The prayer of a righteous man is powerful and effective'* (James 5:16).

We also know that, *'Before they call I will answer; while they are still speaking I will hear'* (Isaiah 65:24).

My wife Susan and I were visiting Hebron Evangelical Church in Carlisle some years ago to share about our work with MAF. We had attended the church in the late 1960s and they had supported us when we went overseas with MAF in 1972. We hadn't been there for about 20 years.

After the service, two ladies came up to us separately and both told us that they had prayed for us every day since we had joined MAF. This was more than 20 years later!

They did not know our every need in Ethiopia nor what to pray for on many occasions, so how effective were their prayers?

Here are two examples:

The first was in the early hours of 13 January 1976 in Jimma, Ethiopia, when Susan gave birth to our third daughter, Sara. There was no reliable local doctor but the birth itself went well. Susan was attended by another pilot's wife, Joyce, who was a midwife, plus a nurse from another mission.

However, Sara took what seemed like a long time to breathe due to her airways being clogged.

Eventually all was okay, but then Susan developed a problem which threatened her life. It was really touch and go for a while whether she would live, but at 1.30 in the morning we managed to get advice from a doctor 200 miles away. I quickly headed off to the local hospital where I was able to collect the necessary drug that was to save Susan's life.

The second occasion was a year later when I flew to a destination in south-east Ethiopia where there was a lot of rebel activity. The flight was uneventful and I collected the passengers and returned to Addis Ababa.

Some days afterwards, I learned that rebels in that area had known the MAF plane was coming and had made plans to 'meet the plane' at the airport and capture the pilot. They arrived after I had left and were so angry they had missed the plane that they opened fire on the local town and burned many buildings.

Was it my desperate prayers that night as I saw my wife at death's door and imagined me returning to the UK as a widower with three small girls to care for? Or was it the prayers of those two ladies in Carlisle and many others like them? I believe it was combination of them all!

Without the prayers of friends like the ladies from Carlisle, life would be impossible for us in MAF. I am very aware that there are many occasions when God listens to pray-ers who have no idea what they were praying for.

And this leads me on to another issue. Many missions, MAF included, have people working in very sensitive situations and difficult countries where the need for absolute security is paramount. The work cannot be described and sometimes the workers themselves cannot be identified. MAF has situations like that.

In those situations we rely totally on people who will pray and be able to support such work without the satisfaction of knowing what that work is, what the needs are, or whether their prayers have been answered.

How do you pray? Is it a regular and faithful prayer for God's work even when you don't know the specific need? Do you pray 'not knowing what for, or why?' but trusting God to answer your prayers for His saints wherever and whatever they are doing?

Your prayers can be powerful and effective!

*Max Gove*
*Special Projects Manager*

# 'Flying Blind'

If you look inside the cockpit of an aircraft you will see many different instruments, dials, switches and knobs. As complicated as they might seem, many of them are simply designed to replace the information that a pilot loses when there is no visibility through the cockpit windows – allowing them to 'fly blind'.

None of the individual instruments could do this job alone – the pilot has to use all the instruments in combination. But if the pilot is not trained how to interpret the information from all those instruments, the information they provide is useless.

Pilots who don't have an instrument flying licence may know all the instruments and the information each of them provides, but without proper training and practice, they will struggle to survive in 'blind flying' conditions.

A crisis in your life is not the place where you begin to learn how to deal with it. You have to learn your lessons before you actually need them.

Through my life God has always challenged me. He started with small challenges, but the challenges grew. So as I got older I was able to navigate through some really dark nights, because I knew that I could rely on what the Lord had taught me. I know many people are, at best, annoyed or even angry when God puts challenges in front of them, but how else can we learn?

It all starts with God showing us in so many ways how He loves us, yet we fail to see or understand it. Sometimes, it takes someone else to point out the blessings in our lives.

When things start to become harder, it does not mean that God wants to give us a hard time just for the sake of it; on the contrary, He feels that we are up to bigger challenges, not for our sake – but for His.

God is building His Kingdom and He needs qualified staff for all sorts of tasks. Pilots who 'fly blind' don't usually do it for the fun of it, but to fulfil what is on the passengers' agenda. When challenged to work for God, I want to be trained and ready.

'Then I heard the Lord asking, "Whom should I send as a messenger to this people? Who will go for us?" I said, "Here I am. Send me!"'

(Isaiah 6:8)

*Jakob Adolf*
*Pilot – Madagascar and South Sudan*

# Perseverance

*'Therefore, since we are surrounded by such a great cloud of witnesses, let us throw off everything that hinders and the sin that so easily entangles, and let us run with perseverance the race marked out for us.'*

(Hebrews 12:1)

My sons play chess and my 11-year-old, William, lost a game recently after having been on quite a winning streak. He was devastated and came to me after the game, barely holding back the tears.

He immediately announced that he'd had enough and didn't want to play chess anymore. I reminded him that he was committed to the school team for the year, but if he still wanted to give up at the end of the year, he was free to do so then.

Soon after, he played in a chess tournament and finished the day having won six out of his seven games (and having drawn the seventh one). After this success, all talk of giving up was gone.

He told me quite philosophically that he'd just got out of practice at losing, but that he was learning again and was going to be good at it – so long as he didn't have to do it too often!

I can certainly relate to William's sentiments. It's all too easy to want to give up when the going gets tough. When we face obstacles in our ministry – when the price of Avgas soars, when local governments are obstructive, when riots or rebel activity threaten us, when unreliable infrastructures delay us, and even when our co-workers frustrate us, it is natural to want to throw in the towel.

But God has not given us a spirit of defeatism. He calls us to persevere! He calls us to overcome! We need to throw off the negative attitudes of discouragement and despair.

Yes, we'll face setbacks. Yes, it's often tough. But if Jesus has marked out our path, if Jesus is directing our ministry, and if we are living and working in His strength, we will succeed!

*Angela Harding*
*Legal and Communications Officer, MAF Asia Pacific*

# Just One Word

We moved to Kampala, Uganda, having lived in Chad for four years in our first posting with MAF.

I would love to be able to say that the transition was easy but, strangely, once we arrived in Uganda, the desert and uncomfortable climate of Chad screamed out to my very being to go back – to return to the familiar, to the friendships, to the local Chadians who had got under our skin and, to the simplicity of life there.

The scream was not only to me but to my three children as well, who occasionally reminded me of our betrayal in abandoning Chad for the green hills of Kampala. We moved to Kampala after wrestling with God over the decision; knowing that our eldest child needed a good English secondary school and that Uganda's operation was busy and in need of another pilot.

When I asked the Lord for a direct word (with a clear reference so I could be sure I would know it was Him speaking), I heard Him say quietly, 'Read Ezekiel 37:13-15.'

It read, '*And you shall know that I am the Lord, when I have opened your graves, O my people, and brought you up out of your graves and shall put My Spirit in you and you shall live, and I shall place you in your own land: then shall you know that I the Lord have spoken it and performed it, says the Lord.*'

Chad's chequered history had made it literally an open graveyard. The suggestion of 'our own land' made me feel as though we would make Uganda our home. I really had to stop wrestling at this point and just obey.

Chad had become, after a long time of various trials, a place where we felt fulfilled. We had come to see what a treasure God gave us when He called us to go there in 2007. I yet again had debated with God, telling Him every reason under the sun why I wasn't suited to such a place. But God was quite clear. Again, He gave a direct reference from Jeremiah 42 telling us to not disobey His direction as things would be worse for us in the very place where we thought life would be safer and easier (13-17). But if we obeyed His voice, He would be with us and protect and provide for us (10-12).

The week before we had to leave England, I lay awake crying out to Him not to make me go. I really felt incapable of dealing with the heat of Chad, let alone the inhospitable place I'd seen it to be when I first visited there a few months before.

This time, I felt Him draw close and whisper yet again more comforting verses from Jeremiah 17:8, which read, '*You shall be like a tree planted by the waters which spreads out her roots by the river* (N'Djaména has a river running through it!) *and shall not fear when heat comes, but her leaf shall be green; and shall not be anxious in the year of drought, neither shall cease from yielding fruit.*'

My spine tingled as I read the Scripture with the wonder of how His Word was more relevant than anything any human could have spoken into my heart. It touched on every fear that was deep inside of me – our God knows the deepest part of us.

He alone can speak one word and the storm inside of us can be stilled. One word from Him is enough to chase all fears away and girds us with a faith that can step out in utter abandonment to a Lord who promises He will carry us, and will never leave us or forsake us.

When I look back at my deep longing for Chad, my awareness of what a treasure that place was to us as a family – I realise that God was in that place with us, along with many other people who went there because He asked them to, and know that I cannot wrestle with Him any longer.

I don't know how God will use me in Uganda and in the years to come; I feel very small and invisible being among people who don't know me and who I don't know. But I know that God always has a purpose and He is to be trusted.

If God is calling you to do something you feel unable to do, or you think is virtually impossible, it will probably turn out to be the greatest blessing of your life. If we just abide in Him, He will do the rest.

If we say like Isaiah, 'Here I am Lord, send me!' He will do the sending. If we say, 'I surrender to you, Lord', He will take us and use us in ways we never dreamed possible.

Life is never dull with the Lord... it is one extreme adventure after another.

*Jill Vine*
*Uganda Information Officer*

# When God Wants a Job Done

*'Then have them make a sanctuary for me, and I will dwell among them. Make this tabernacle and all its furnishings exactly like the pattern I will show you.'*

(Exodus 25:8-9)

God had an important job He wanted done. He wanted the children of Israel to build a sanctuary for Him so He could live among the people. He gave Moses a very detailed description and plan of how He wanted the sanctuary to be built and for all its furnishings.

These included the ark of the testimony, the table, the lampstand, the tabernacle, the altar of burnt offering, the courtyard, oil for the lampstand, the priestly garments, the ephod and the breastplate.

I wonder how Moses felt as God went through this long list detailing exactly how it should be made. I wonder if he thought, 'Hold on, Lord, this is too much for me to take in and exactly how do you expect me to do all this?' However, God was not asking him to 'go it alone', but gave him people to work with him on the project.

The people were Bezalel, Oholiab and a team of craftsmen. God had given Moses the big picture and a team of people to work out the detail. Bezalel was skilled in all kinds of crafts, to make artistic designs for work in gold, silver and bronze, to cut and set stones and to work in wood. Then there was Oholiab, who was appointed to help him, along with a team of craftsmen to make everything God had commanded.

However, Bezalel was not only an extremely skilled craftsman but, more importantly, he was filled with the Spirit of God, he was anointed for the task. He was probably chosen because he had a desire to use his skills to honour God and bless the people.

We all have gifts, talents and skills that we can bring to be used by God. Some of these are obvious for all to see because we use them all the time. Some may yet be hidden, but will be revealed as they are needed. The important thing is that we have a desire to use them for the honour of God and to bless His people.

Let's daily bring ourselves and what we do under the anointing of God for Him to use for His glory in whatever way He chooses.

God not only gives us a job to do but He also equips us to do it.

*Margaret Simpson*
*Finance Officer*

# Desert Times

*'Now an angel of the Lord spoke to Philip, saying, "Arise and go toward the south along the road which goes down from Jerusalem to Gaza."'*

(Acts 8:26)

Philip may have felt a little confused...

He had been appointed to be a deacon in Jerusalem. What a privileged position to be called to this task and to complement the work of the apostles! But then, as a result of sadness and persecution, he next finds himself in a different kind of ministry in Samaria.

This ends up becoming a blessed and exciting time. But he is then whisked away to the desert road − where nothing happens.

That is what the wilderness is like. All the familiar supports are stripped away. It is not an easy place to be − but then the Ethiopian comes along.

Philip hears what the Ethiopian is saying and knows that he can respond to this need. A person's life is changed. Perhaps many other people's lives are going to be changed because of this encounter.

There may be times in our lives when we feel we have moved, or been moved, perhaps unexpectedly, to the desert. We have been taken away from good things. We are no longer involved or contributing, we have been taken to... nothing.

No status or ministry, and missing out on all the exciting or comforting things that are happening elsewhere. Just sitting by the side of the road − it appears to make no sense. It can be very tough and confusing, but it was a pattern for a large number of biblical heroes. A time in the wilderness was part of God's plan.

God knows about timing, and someone needed to be in that desert place to meet the traveller.

Philip ministered to the Ethiopian, and then left the desert. Wilderness times do not last for ever.

What have been the desert times in your life?

What did you learn about yourself in those times? What was God doing in you, for your own sake and for the sake of others? (You may also want to read Acts 6:5, 8:4-8, 8:26-40.)

**Prayer:**

Heavenly Father, we do not know who will cross our path today. May we stay obedient to You as You prepare us to meet them – whoever they will be, wherever we will be. May we listen and seek to show them Christ's love. Amen.

*Rev Anthony Buckley*
*MAF UK Trustee*

# The Inspiration of Ol' Camel Knees

I was thinking of Elijah yesterday – that scene where he was on Mount Carmel after the big Baal blowout, and he was praying for rain. How many times did he send his servant to look for a result? And how many years had he waited for God's perfect moment, even though his own life was in danger the whole time because of his stand?

Come to think of it, James was impressed with Elijah. The apostle James knew what it was like to be human. He also knew what it meant to persevere in prayer, and he holds Elijah up as an example: 'The prayer of a person living right with God is something powerful to be reckoned with'.

Elijah, for instance, human just like us, prayed hard that it wouldn't rain, and it didn't – not a drop for 3½ years. Then he prayed that it would rain and it did. The showers came and everything started growing again.

James completely skips over the whole public Baal thing – he focuses on the two bookends of hard, private prayer.

James was a pastor. He makes some bold statements about prayer in the other chapters of his letter. Often these assertions don't line up with my personal experience. I want to be effective in prayer, so what does it take?

Back to Elijah... There he was on Mount Carmel. The idolaters had been defeated. He climbed to the top of the mountain (been there, done that). Then he 'bent down to the ground and put his face between his knees.' Oh, that's it – that's why I'm so ineffective at praying! I can't get my face between my knees. (Better only try that if you're at home.)

Now just wait a minute. Is it about posture? Yes? No? I think it is. It's about how we stand, kneel or fall on our face before God. When was the last time you were really desperate that God would answer your cry? What did you do? Can I take a guess?

When we are desperate – and we come to the place of knowing that God is our only hope, I believe our posture changes (inside at least). Acknowledging our small-ness in front of His great-ness ensures that we live according to His way. The result is obvious; we will be 'living right with God'.

Eugene Peterson was also a pastor. I think he has a soft spot for James. In his introduction to the book of James in *The Message* he chose to include the church tradition that 'James carried the nickname 'Old Camel Knees' because of thick calluses built up on his knees from many years of determined praying.'

Am I willing to sacrifice my knees to achieve small-ness?

*Keith Ketchum*
*Maintenance Manager, Africa Region*

# Having the Right Attitude

*'Your attitude should be that of Christ Jesus.'*
(Philippians 2:1-8)

Another knock on the gate, another request for financial help, a friend in crisis, the tug of a child on my legs and yet one more call to the power or water company to try and get my supply switched on.

There are many days when the busyness and frustrations of life in Uganda seem endless. To someone on the outside, I probably appear to be doing all the things one would expect of someone who is serving the Lord full-time on the mission field, and I do it with a smile on my face – most of the time!

I pray with that friend in crisis. I give when I feel the Lord has led me to give. I spend many hours giving hospitality to those who visit. I may be doing all the right things and yet, my heart and mind may not be in the right place. I can be resentful of intrusions on my time or lack genuine compassion for a person.

However, serving one another is not all that God's Word commands of us. As Paul writes to the Philippians, he makes it clear that we should *'Do everything without complaining or arguing'*. Our attitudes (minds) should be that of Christ Jesus, who not only took on the actions of a servant, but took on 'the very nature of a servant'. In humility, He sacrificed everything.

I am not there yet! I do not always act out of humility or selflessness. I am not always able to sacrifice everything. However, the examples of people like Paul and Timothy assure me that this command is possible, and I pray each day that I would grow to be more like Christ in attitude, as well as action.

*Sarah Newnham*
*MAF Uganda*

# Making a Pit Stop with the Lord each Day

I am a big Formula 1 fan and it always fascinates me just how much some of the sport has changed over the years. When it started in the 1950s, if a car came in for a pit stop to refuel and change tyres, a couple of mechanics would do the work, the driver might get out of the car, stretch his legs or have a quick drink or a smoke – then off he would go.

Whereas nowadays, the car comes into the pits and a team of around 19 people descend on it to do everything they need to do in around 3 seconds. They have three people on each wheel, three doing the fuel, and the driver certainly wouldn't even consider getting out unless the race was over.

They also have another group of people monitoring all the aspects of the car, and of the race itself, in order to best advise the driver when to make a pit stop. But even with all this meticulous planning, the teams still don't manage to get it right and win every time.

We can experience this same problem in our daily life too. Under our own ideas and plans, even though we might strive for something, plan it so carefully and aim to be the best, we still fall short. However, as Christians we are able to turn to an awesome God. But we shouldn't just turn to Him once things have started going wrong. We need to try to walk along the route He has laid out for us to begin with, to talk with Him as often as possible, not just when we think we need Him.

> *"'For I know the plans I have for you,' declares the Lord, "plans to prosper you and not to harm you, plans to give you hope and a future."'*
>
> (Jeremiah 29:11)

This promise belongs to each one of us, and we need to believe it and try to live every day of our lives within His plan. If not, then we can expect to always have a little niggle at the back of our minds that we aren't quite fulfilled.

When we let God have the steering wheel of our lives He is able to fulfil His plans for us. If He calls us to be something the world sees as mundane, then He will have given us all the gifts we need to excel at our calling, and to be fulfilled by it.

If we choose to go against the calling because we feel we want 'something more' or are ashamed of what the world will think of us, then no matter how much training we do or effort we put in, we might achieve our aim, but we will never feel truly fulfilled.

God told Jeremiah, *'Before I formed you in the womb I knew you, before you were born I set you apart'* (Jeremiah 1:5). Like Jeremiah, we have been set apart. We aren't supposed to imitate anyone else, we are called to be all that God wants us to be.

In Ephesians 2:10 it is written, *'For we are God's workmanship, created in Christ Jesus to do good works, which God prepared in advance for us to do.'* When He created you He gave you everything you would need to fulfil your purpose. We each need to seek Him daily in order to develop those skills during our lifetime. If we just seek God when we are in times of trouble, it will take us much longer to develop our skills to their full potential.

Hebrews 11:6 says, *'You can never please God without faith, without depending on Him. Anyone who wants to come to God must believe that there is a God and that He rewards those who sincerely look for Him.'* We must all realise that there is no way that we can improve God's plan for us. The gift that Jesus gave us allows us the connection with God that we need, to live a life for Him — rich in His blessings.

> *'You will seek me and find me when you seek me with all your heart.'*
>
> (Jeremiah 29:13)

**Prayer:**

Lord, I believe that You created each one of us for a special purpose, and that You have a perfect plan for our lives. I ask that You fulfil Your purpose for each one of us, as we try to do our part by earnestly seeking You daily, through prayer and through Your Word, and by trusting in You and not in our own ideas and desires. We pray that as we seek You each day, You will *'guide us along the best pathway for our lives'*.

(Psalm 32:8)

*Stephen Rayner, Supporter Relations*

# God's Messengers

*"I will send my messenger ahead of you, who will prepare your way – a voice of one calling in the wilderness, 'Prepare the way for the Lord, make straight paths for Him.'" And so John the Baptist appeared in the wilderness, preaching a baptism of repentance for the forgiveness of sins. The whole Judean countryside and all the people of Jerusalem went out to him. Confessing their sins, they were baptised by him in the Jordan River.'*

(Mark 1:2-5)

Although the Lord can do all things, He has throughout history used His messengers to point the way towards His Son Jesus and salvation. MAF is part of a long tradition of being Christ's messengers, and like John the Baptist, much of MAF's ministry is carried out in desert places, isolated places, places of solitude due to geography.

Flying into such hard-to-reach places, MAF planes are welcomed by crowds of people – a bit like Jesus and His messengers when they arrived in a new area. The people then, and the people now, are in need. They're in need of truth and they're in need of help – both of which can be found in Jesus.

Over 2,000 years ago, the disciples were boatmen and fishermen, called to use their technical skills to transport Jesus to people living in different places. Reaching those in need remains paramount, and today MAF uses modern-day methods to take God's love and His message of salvation to those who have yet to hear the Good News.

I believe the message is this: if we are prepared to 'Go' and be the Lord's messengers, to share His love and prepare the way for God to bless His people, then we will come across those who want to hear, are ready to hear, and are willing to respond – no matter how remote those places may be!

Let us continue daily to be messengers for Christ. Whether we need to cross the sea or simply the street, may we see people living in physical or geographical isolation find the one true God and be set free by His love.

*Dr Ian Harnett, MAF UK Trustee*

# Worry Wednesday

*'Can any one of you by worrying add a single hour to your life?'*

(Matthew 6:27)

As Bill and I flew on a commercial flight from Australia to Papua New Guinea (PNG) to attend our international staff's annual conference, I listened to a sermon on my iPod called 'From worry to worship'.

Since I struggle with worry, I was immediately intrigued. The speaker shared about a man who gave himself permission to worry, but only one day a week.

On every day of the week except Wednesday, he would write down any worry that came to mind, put it in a box and leave it until 'Worry Wednesday'. Then, with the worry put aside for the time being, he would worship God.

When 'Worry Wednesday' came, he would open the box and find that the vast majority of things that he had been tempted to worry about had already been and gone.

I've put this into practice over the last few days and have been amazed at how it's working. I'm giving myself permission to worry, but just not yet. I was tempted to worry about whether my sons would be safe while we were away.

Because we were in PNG from Thursday to Monday, it didn't get to 'Worry Wednesday' until I was home to find them safe and well. I wanted to worry about whether I'd get eaten by sharks while snorkelling off the Madang coast. (Yes, it's a tough life being a missionary – sometimes!)

But I didn't even have time to write that worry down, let alone get to 'Worry Wednesday', before I was back on shore – with all my limbs.

I am discovering that if, instead of worrying, I focus first on God, His sovereignty, power and love, then worrying somehow becomes unnecessary.

I hope that yours is a worry-free week this week – even Wednesday.

*Angela Harding*
*Legal and Communications Officer, MAF Asia Pacific*

# We Bothered

*'Three times I was beaten with rods. Once I was stoned. Three times I was shipwrecked; a night and a day I was adrift at sea; on frequent journeys, in danger from rivers, danger from robbers, danger from my own people, danger from Gentiles, danger in the city, danger in the wilderness, danger at sea, danger from false brothers; in toil and hardship, through many a sleepless night, in hunger and thirst, often without food, in cold and exposure. And, apart from other things, there is the daily pressure on me of my anxiety for all the churches. Who is weak, and I am not weak? Who is made to fall, and I am not indignant?'*

(2 Corinthians 11:25-29)

Some years ago in Uganda we had an emergency call from a Christian medical team. They were working in some villages in the Semliki district, on the southern shore of Lake Albert, carrying out dental and medical work. They had come across many difficult medical cases, but one they felt they might be able to help was urgent – a young 14-year-old girl with kidney failure.

I had been flying the MAF floatplane on Lake Victoria and the call came as I was on my way back to base. We worked out that there was just enough time to swap aircraft and make it to Semliki, have half an hour on the ground and make it back before last landing time.

I headed out for the hour's flight and was surprised at how horrible the weather was to the west as it had been very pleasant over the lake. I had to sneak under the low cloud that had formed around the hills and then dropped down onto the dirt airstrip.

Then, to my surprise, when we shut down we came under attack from tsetse flies. They dive-bombed the aircraft, sounding like hail as they pinged off the fuselage. They can give a nasty bite, so I decided to stay in the aircraft until the team arrived as I was wearing shorts – something I only ever did when flying the floatplane as one often gets a tad damp.

The medical team arrived and we gently lowered the young girl onto the stretcher in our small aircraft with her mother. We smiled, prayed for them, and then took off into what I can only describe as horrendous weather. I really wanted to get through; otherwise I would have to return and stay overnight, which, with such a sick patient, would not be good.

Much to my relief and thankfulness there was a gap in the clouds. I nipped through it and headed back to Kajjansi, MAF's airstrip near Kampala. Sadly, the doctors could do little for the girl and she slipped away a few days later, but I was taken by what the mother said, 'Why did you bother helping us?'

Well, from my experience as a Christian (which at my age is quite extensive!) the answer was simple... because that is exactly what disciples of Christ are meant to do – we're meant to bother.

***Prayer:***

Heavenly Father, when life's situations, circumstances or simple tiredness cause me not to want to bother – may I remember Paul and all the people he helped and all the lives that were changed because he bothered to follow you wholeheartedly – regardless of all he had gone through. May I never grow weary in sharing and showing Your love. May I always be willing to go to the ends of the earth in my service for You. Amen.

*Bryan Pill*
*Pilot – Uganda & Chad*

# Calm for the Frazzled Soul

I do not consider myself to be a calm person. My wife and daughter often remind me to 'chill out'.

No doubt we can all echo this feeling from time to time. Some of us are aware that our very natures conspire against us as we seek to move things forward at work, church or home. I was rather un-calm when I first joined MAF due to the fact that my wife and I needed to sell our house.

An added pressure was that we required the council to provide a building certificate for a garage conversion. Both the council and builder moved at a snail's pace.

Going through the gamut of emotions we experience with life's daily challenges, I am brought back to sanity with four elements of God's provision in Philippians 4:4-7. We start with the encouragement to *'Rejoice in the Lord always'* (verse 4). And to make quite sure we did hear that correctly – *'I will say it again: Rejoice!'* We have so much to be thankful for. Being thankful helps us to get those challenges into perspective, to bring us back to the heart of worshipping and adoring the Lord.

Yet, in everyday life, how do I respond to those people who agitate me? What behaviour is being observed of me? The apostle prompts us to *'Let your gentleness be evident to all'* (verse 5). We live in a world where there is so much harshness and aggression. As Christians we need to exhibit that characteristic of gentleness – perhaps it is harder for men.

After the two aspects about what we should do, the Lord now gives us two assurances in our frazzled state. *'Do not be anxious about anything'* (verse 6). This verse almost indicates that we should be irresponsible, but it comes with a condition that we pray about our needs with a thankful heart. We need to accept that the Lord is with us in our circumstances and that we have not been abandoned.

And lastly, to bring the soothing balm to the troubled heart – *'the peace of God will guard your hearts and your minds in Christ Jesus'* (verse 7). It is like peace being our guide and guard as we move forward in faith.

Time and time again, in those troubled times, the Lord has provided that peace when I needed His assurance on those not so calm days.

Today, if you find yourself frazzled – know the Lord is your calm!

*Gary Colvin*
*MAF UK Head of Human Resources*

# Modern Day Gatekeepers

*'The gatekeepers guarded the gates and did not need to leave their post of duty for their meals were brought to them.'*

(2 Chronicles 35:15)

This verse fascinates me. It is the fact that the gatekeepers had their meals brought to them, which emphasises how important their positions were; they couldn't even leave their posts to go and eat. Gatekeepers needed to be on duty at all times.

The more I think about it, the more I begin to realise that we need to become modern day gatekeepers. Be that gatekeepers for our lives, our families or, in the case of MAF, gatekeepers for our overseas staff.

Whether we realise it or not, we are already undertaking gatekeeper duties in our working lives. The first thing gatekeepers do is stand watch and offer protection. At MAF we can help guard and protect those on the field by praying for them.

Gatekeepers also 'shout the news', which is done through our magazine *Flying for Life*, on the website and in other forms of communication.

Another duty of the gatekeeper is to care for the articles used in worship. We can link this to how MAF provides finance for the maintenance of our airplanes – definitely a case of looking after things that are used to worship and glorify God.

Finally, gatekeepers collect money and gifts, must be reliable, trustworthy and, most importantly, they are there to serve.

Returning to the point of 'meals being brought' and how gatekeepers were constantly on guard, I think that is where the real challenge lies.

In order for us to fully take up the responsibility of being gatekeepers, we must commit to being on duty at all times, and so live out 1 Thessalonians 5:17 and 'pray without ceasing'.

Like the Levites who carried out their duties inside the temple, safe in the knowledge that the gatekeepers were guarding the entrance, our overseas staff also need to have that confidence that we as MAF staff and prayer supporters are keeping a constant watch over them.

So the challenge for me is not just am I willing to be an MAF gatekeeper with all that it entails, but am I also prepared that this is not a part-time position, but one – like any vital role – that requires constant dedication?

**Prayer:**

Heavenly Father, may we keep our eyes fixed upon You and remain diligent in prayer as we continue looking to protect all You have entrusted to us, to care for, oversee and nurture in our lives.

*Sam Oliver*
*Events Officer*

# Forgiveness

The Jews taught that a man was to forgive another three times, but not the fourth.

We read in Matthew 18:21 that Peter said to Jesus, *'How many times shall I forgive my brother when he sins against me?'* In Matthew 18:22 Jesus says, '70 times 7' in the NKJ, which is recorded as '77 times' in the NIV. He didn't mean that we are to forgive only 490 or 77 times!

While I was flying as an MAF pilot in Ethiopia from 1972-77, I got to know many people. One such was Heikki – a missionary from Finland. I met up with Heikki again in 1994 when he told me this story.

Heikki's mission had an evangelism initiative in the villages in Sidamo Province south of Addis Ababa. In Ethiopia at that time there was a major faith vacuum after the overthrow of communism.

One day, a missionary colleague was driving south to preach in the villages in that area. As he drove through a small town, a 12-year-old girl ran out in front of his vehicle and was killed. There are always serious implications in fatal accidents in Africa – most people wouldn't stop but would drive to the nearest police station. But on this occasion the driver stopped.

The parents of the young girl and the town elders wanted the matter settled in the 'traditional way' and asked him to bring his mission leader down from Addis Ababa.

Heikki and the missionary made a special visit to the village. There was a crowd waiting. A mat was laid out on the ground and the driver was asked to sit down with the girl's parents on the mat. A blanket was put across their shoulders, joining them together, and a meal was brought for them to share.

After they had eaten, the father got up and announced that the matter of his daughter's death was forgiven, forgotten and should never be spoken of again. The village elder also spoke. He said, 'In addition, all are reconciled as from tonight and the matter must never be spoken of again by anyone here.'

He also said to Heikki and the missionary, 'You have become our relatives and are now part of our family.'

Have you ever known forgiveness like that?

The Bible speaks about God offering that kind of forgiveness in the following Scriptures:

◊   Hebrews 8:12: *'I will remember their sins no more.'*

◊   Ephesians 1:7-8: *'In Him we have redemption through His blood, the forgiveness of sins, in accordance with the riches of God's grace that He lavished on us with all wisdom and understanding.'*

◊   Colossians 1:13-14: *'For He has rescued us from the dominion of darkness and brought us into the Kingdom of the Son He loves, in whom we have redemption, the forgiveness of sins.'*

◊   Colossians 1:21-22: *'Once you were alienated from God and were enemies in your minds because of your evil behaviour. But now He has reconciled you by Christ's physical body through death to present you holy in His sight, without blemish and free from accusation.'*

◊   1 John 1:8-9: *'If we say that we have no sin, we are deceiving ourselves and the truth is not in us. If we confess our sins, He is faithful and righteous to forgive us our sins and to cleanse us from all unrighteousness.'*

Do you really know that kind of forgiveness from God?

Too many people say, and even some Christians believe, 'But God could never forgive me for that sin'. Have you thought what that says about the Lord Jesus Christ? It is actually saying that God's supreme sacrifice, the death of His only beloved Son, was not sufficient to cover this sin or that sin!

There's more! The first instance of the word forgive (*nasa/nasah* – to send away a person's punishment) is found in Genesis 50:15-17.

Joseph's brothers were very worried when their father Jacob died, thinking that Joseph would now seek retribution for their treatment of him many years before. So they probably misrepresented their father by saying to Joseph that Jacob had asked them to tell Joseph to forgive this moral debt entirely – to release them from the just penalty they deserved.

Joseph didn't question the source but took the action of absolving them, agreeing to impose no further punishment.

It is important to remember that forgiveness is an action – the action of releasing someone from their deserved punishments and obligations. It is not an emotion or a feeling; it is an intentional act of deciding to grant full absolution to one who does not deserve it.

It is the action of surrendering one's rights to be compensated, or to be given reparation, or to seek rightful civil punishment against another who has wronged you.

Forgiveness is an action. If you know and love the Lord Jesus Christ, you have received unconditional forgiveness from God because of Jesus dying in your place. But have you given that unconditional forgiveness to others? To those in your family, to those where you work, to your neighbour or to a fellow Christian?

I know Christians who say they can 'never' forgive. Or will 'only forgive if that person does this or that...' But on what basis do they offer that kind of forgiveness? It is not the example shown to us by our heavenly Father. As Christians we have been forgiven unconditionally by God, so while we praise Him for our forgiveness, we must be willing to extend that unconditional forgiveness to others. For more, see Matthew 18:23-30.

Back to the end of Heikki's story...

Heikki took the opportunity to reply, 'You have said that we are family so I will visit with you and stop for a meal whenever I pass through this village.' Heikki began regular visits to the man, his wife and their children.

On his first visit on a Friday, Heikki asked, 'May I stop on my way home to Addis Ababa on Monday to eat and pray with you?' He did this on a regular basis whenever travelling south and one day gave a copy of the New Testament as a gift to the father, encouraging him to read it.

After some visits, the father said that he read from the New Testament before going to the fields each day and prayed to Jesus. He said that it made him feel good. Heikki told him to keep reading! While in Finland, another missionary took Heikki's place and eventually led the whole family to Christ. The whole family were baptised.

I got this update later from Heikki in 2004: 'Since the father's commitment to follow Jesus Christ, he has given land for the building of a church. He is now a church elder and many others in the village have become Christians.

'In the whole area in the past 4 years over 4,000 people have become Christians and there are approximately 100-150 baptisms every 3 months.'

*Max Gove*
*Special Projects Manager*

# Taking the Risk

*'Whoever desires to come after Me, let him deny himself, and take up his cross, and follow Me. For whoever desires to save his life will lose it, but whoever loses his life for My sake and the Gospel's will save it. For what will it profit a man if he gains the whole world, and loses his own soul?'*

(Mark 8:34-36)

Having lived in the UK and Papua New Guinea (PNG) for nearly 20 years, it is hard not to notice the difference in attitudes to 'risk' in both countries. In PNG, I see children, barely more than toddlers, carrying bush knives nearly as long as they are tall, which makes me wonder, 'What are their parents thinking about?'

And then there are the parents themselves, walking across wet, slippery logs which serve as a bridge, with nothing either side, crossing a deep ravine filled with a rushing torrent of water. There's also the motorised method of transportation – bus drivers speeding up to claim whichever side of the road belongs to them. Or the number of people who cram on or into the buses as they speed away in a trail of dust!

And then there is MAF in PNG. The short, steep, slippery airstrips we land on every day are hardly normal as far as global aviation regards normal. Even though we do all we can to keep our flights safe, a risk is involved.

The UK is now incredibly risk averse, afraid that an injury just might occur, or that something might just go wrong. Fear paralyses: fear of risk; fear of failure; fear of litigation; fear of doing wrong. Inaction and lost opportunities follow the fear.

However, Jesus calls us to take a risk and follow Him. He demands priority over money, possessions and relationships – including strong and legitimate family bonds. He speaks strongly in what He says to people who say they'll follow Him, but then look back at what they've left behind. Then there's the parable about how riches and worldly cares affect our productivity in the Kingdom of God.

Jesus speaks about endurance, meaning that the road can be long and tiring. He speaks about perseverance, meaning that the road can be difficult and needs effort and determination. He speaks about victory and joy, meaning that the journey is more than worth it.

Many times, people have said to me, 'I do admire what you're doing, but I could never do that.' Maybe not, as God has given me my own set of skills to serve him with. However, what about the risk of following Jesus? Yes, this is for us all – equally – and with the Lord's same set of demands and challenges, along with the same privilege, joy and glorious hope before us. Be certain, however, it is not for the faint-hearted and neither is it without risk.

If I can dare to paraphrase Jesus:

> 'Take a risk! Live dangerously! Follow Me out of your protective
> and secure comfort zones. Embrace whatever difficulties come
> your way as a result of following Me. I'll be with you through
> them all and in the process you'll gain true life. Don't lose
> your life in possessions and money – they will steal your soul.
> Remember, one day, you will have to give an account of whether
> you took the risk of following Me, or not.'

Let us trust the Lord in all He calls us to do.

*Michael Duncalfe*
*Pilot – Papua New Guinea*

# Hope in the Lord

*'Those who hope in the Lord will renew their strength. They will soar on wings like eagles; they will run and not grow weary, they will walk and not be faint.'*

(Isaiah 40:31)

Even the strongest people get tired and frightened at times, but God's power and strength never diminish. He is never tired or too busy to help and listen. His strength is our source of strength. When you feel that life is crushing you and you cannot go another step, remember that you can call upon God to renew your strength.

This passage, and the prayers and support from the MAF family, were very special to me during my journey through cancer surgery and radiotherapy treatment. It is a wonderful reminder of where our strength really comes from. It helped to lift me and to keep me focused during my illness. This passage also put many things in perspective, because the source of our strength and abilities doesn't come from us or anything we have done, but rather it is all from the Lord God.

For me, 'hoping in the Lord', is expecting that His promise of strength will help me to rise above life's distractions and difficulties. It means trusting in God. Trusting in God also helps us to be prepared when He speaks to us. Then we will be patient when He asks us to wait, and expect Him to fulfil the promises found in His Word.

Nothing is impossible with God, and no matter how much I am hurting or think that I can't go on, I know that if I trust and rely on Him, I can get through anything.

The same principles apply to the rest of our lives. There are times when we just want to give up; when things are so hard and seem almost unbearable, and we do not think that we are going to get through the challenges and hardships we are facing.

It is in these moments that we must realise that if we are willing to surrender, trust and rely on Jesus, there isn't anything He cannot get us through. The prophet Isaiah tells us today that *'God does not grow faint or weary'*, and those who put their hope in Him will not either.

I learnt three things through this time:

**God should be our only source of hope** – I have sometimes kept my hope in someone or something other than God. However, Jehoshaphat prayed in 2 Chronicles 20:12, *'Our eyes are set upon You; You are our only hope'*. And we read in Psalm 25:15, *'My eyes are ever on the Lord, for only He will release my feet from the snare'*.

**We need to spend time alone with God and be still** – Elijah was so discouraged and stressed out, that he left his servant and fled for his life (1 Kings 19:1-9). God wanted to renew His servant's strength, and led him to a cave in the holy mountain, Sinai. Alone in the cave, Elijah's strength to serve God was renewed after a fresh encounter with the Lord. God's renewing grace is best experienced in isolation and stillness.

**Submit to God's sovereignty** – this is what a close Christian friend of mine said to me when I was first diagnosed with cancer. God works in His own time and way (see Isaiah 55:8-9). He works all things towards a goal – the goal He has set for our lives, and He never forsakes us or leaves us behind.

Wait upon the Lord – and you will soar like an eagle!

*Roger Mitty*
*Chairman, MAF UK Board of Trustees*

# Seventy Per Cent

*'And my God shall supply all your need according to His riches in glory by Christ Jesus.'*

(Philippians 4:19)

An African friend of mine, finding herself in a financial pickle, asked the Lord for £10, promising Him 60% back upon receiving the money. The Lord generously provided the money and, deciding to increase her offering, she gave 70% back to Him. In order to place her money in the offering, she bought an item for a pound and made her way to church.

Walking to the grocery store later that afternoon, she thanked the Lord for His provision, but wondered how she was going to manage to buy groceries for the week with only £2.

She proceeded into the store and, with only £2, didn't bother to pick up a basket. As she stood deliberating over what to buy, the shop assistant began placing items on the shelf immediately next to her. When he had finished, he placed a sign above the produce which read, 'Free of charge'. The assistant acknowledged with a smile that it was indeed all free.

Realising the goodness of God, my friend got a trolley and began to fill it with the free items. Bread, fruit, vegetables and other dietary staples, even a large bag of potatoes and a bouquet of flowers went in the trolley. As the assistant looked on, my friend replied that she had a big family – she was thinking of all the others with whom she could share God's provision and blessing.

As I listened to my friend telling me how God provided for her, over and over again she spoke of God's faithfulness. Truly He is faithful.

I smile every time I think of this story, for even with just £2, my friend went shopping, trusted the Lord – not knowing how, but just believing that He would provide – and provide He did, in abundance!

May we trust the Lord in every situation and watch as He supplies all our needs, out of His faithfulness, in His way!

By the way, the £2 was spent on buying bags to carry God's provision home!

*Hilary Brown, Prayer Communications Leader*

# Known by God

*'You have searched me, Lord, and You know me. You know when I sit and when I rise; You perceive my thoughts from afar. You discern my going out and my lying down; You are familiar with all my ways.'*

(Psalm 139:1-3)

When my grandmother moved into a nursing home, my family needed to clear some things from her house. A couple of weeks before this, my father gave me three books from Grandma.

They were books I had never heard of and the bindings were falling apart, but Grandma had specifically asked Dad to give them to me.

I'm not sure why, as she had never mentioned them to me, but Dad said they had meant a lot to her and she wanted me to have them. In the front of each book she had written a note about who had given them to her and when.

For me, these are the most precious things my grandmother has given me from her home, because I love books and I love family history, and one of the books had been given to Grandma by her father.

I always thought that Grandma didn't know me very well, but now I'm thinking that I underestimated her, and she actually knows me quite well!

I am always comforted to know that God knows me, not just quite well, but He really knows me. He knows who I am, what I'm feeling, where my life is going, what I struggle with, what I like – everything about me.

Not only that, He really cares about me too. Whatever is happening in my life, no matter how small, He wants to hear about it.

Today as you go about your daily life, remember that God knows you and He really wants to hear about your day.

Never stop praying!

*Kathryn Smith*
*Funding Co-ordinator*

# Our Choice

*'About midnight Paul and Silas were praying and singing hymns to God.'*

(Acts 16:25)

A few days after cyclone *Yasi* hit the north-eastern coast of Australia just south of where I live, a friend and I began a course at church for those exploring the Christian faith.

We decided to begin the first session asking people to share about their experiences during the cyclone and their view of God in all that happened.

Their comments were revealing and a great starting place for a course that deals with such questions as, 'How can a good God allow bad things to happen?' and, 'Where is God in the midst of suffering?'

But it also made me wonder about my own response. After all, I know that God is good, I know that He loves me, but I also know that bad things happen to 'good' people. That's why, in the run-up to cyclone *Yasi*, I had become a little fatalistic, praying half-heartedly, reasoning that what would happen would happen, and feeling a bit anxious... until a friend rang.

The friend felt led to tell us that we should be worshipping and praising God. And so, in the evening as we waited for cyclone *Yasi* to hit, we sang, we danced and we praised.

I looked up, and when I did, something inside me changed. I felt joy, I had peace, and I was able to sleep.

Graham Kendrick says that, 'Worship is first and foremost for His benefit, not ours, though it is marvellous to discover that in giving Him pleasure, we ourselves enter into what can become our richest and most wholesome experience in life.'

Worshipping God means that what Satan intends for bad in our lives, God is able to use for good. Break-ins, hold-ups, aircraft accidents, illness, loss – nothing is beyond His redemptive power when we choose to worship.

*Angela Harding*
*Legal and Communications Officer, MAF Asia Pacific*

# Understanding God's Word

During a medical visit to Beroroha, Madagascar, we were waiting for the village ladies under a tree on the riverside to do some training about sickness and prevention. I was discussing with the ladies about the health of their children and I asked them what they thought was the cause of sickness and where it came from? All the ladies were really convinced that it is God who brings sickness to their villages.

I started the training by reading Psalm 139 and followed with a short reflection, revealing how God already knew us before we were formed in the womb, and that He loves us, and knows what we need and will provide for us.

After our time of Bible study, I went on to educate the ladies about sickness – highlighting the effects bacteria, germs and viruses have on the body. I then explained that God created the body to fight against disease. I also pointed out that God has given us knowledge as to how we can best prevent sickness and disease through hygiene. One way is simply to wash our hands before we eat.

When the training was finished, one lady shared emotionally that she had just started reading the Bible, but hadn't been able to understand why Jesus healed the people who were sick in the Bible and yet brought sickness to her village.

However, after the Bible study and training, she now understood the stories in the Bible. She then shared with friends and ladies from her own village how big and great God is, and how He loves everyone, and that we shouldn't blame God for sickness.

After she testified about coming to understand what God's Word said, I simply ended the training by saying 'Amen!'

*Corina de Waal*
*MAF South Sudan*

# Into His Arms

*"For I know the plans I have for you," declares the Lord, "plans to prosper you and not to harm you, plans to give you hope and a future."'*

(Jeremiah 29:11)

I can remember my son as a two-year-old, always ready for rough and tumble games, full of life and apparently fearless. I was taking him upstairs to bed one night and as we went, we played. I'm sure those caring for children have experienced the game, 'Okay jump from that step and I will catch you...'

We began playing and he went higher and higher. When he was on stair seven he looked at me and said, 'Daddy, will you catch me? Daddy, please don't drop me.' He leapt and as he flew through the air the look on his face was one of absolute trust. I caught him firmly, and he hugged me, secure in the arms of the one he trusted.

Having visited many MAF operations over the years, I have experienced that level of trust myself. Travelling high above the impassable roads, landing on what can only be described as 'works in progress' – though land we did, bumping to a stop with a sigh of relief.

But there shouldn't have been a sigh – the pilot had prayed for safety for the flight and for his passengers. He had an absolute trust in God.

Knowing the love of God, knowing that our trust is in the One who knows the plans that He has for us, not to harm us but to prosper us, gives us courage, strength and a boldness that enables us all – whether serving with MAF, supporting MAF, or praying for MAF – to continue to face each day resting in His trusting arms.

**Prayer:**

Lord, I thank You for all that You have in store for me and for the MAF team. May our trust in You grow each day as we move into a deeper and more meaningful relationship with You.

*Andy Martin, Community Manager, Scotland*

# Our Daily Bread

*'Give us this day our daily bread.'*

(Luke 11:3)

In Luke chapter 11, the disciples asked Jesus to teach them how to pray. Jesus gave them the Lord's Prayer as a guide and a framework to use for their own personal prayers to God.

In the Lord's Prayer, we see a change of focus in verses 9 and 10. Here the focus is on God – who He is and His desires for His people. Then, in verse 11, the attention is given to the needs of His people.

How often when we pray do we get it the wrong way round – praying for our desires first and often never getting round to acknowledging God and who He is? This is something we must be mindful of. We first need to fix our thoughts on God in our prayer times, and then when we pray for our needs they will be given a proper perspective.

There are occasions when we just need to shoot 'arrow prayers' to heaven, such as 'Help!' but that should not be the extent of our prayer life.

In looking at the word 'bread' in this verse, it doesn't just mean our daily need for food and drink, but anything that supports us in life in serving the Lord. We need to be mindful of what we pray for, but also be mindful of what we will do when God answers our prayer.

God has made us stewards and so we need to be responsible. But when we look at the definition of a steward, what do we see? If we take the example of a flight steward on an aircraft, we realise that their main responsibility is to attend to the needs of the passengers and the flight crew.

God has asked us to be stewards and to manage His affairs on earth in whatever capacity, wherever He has placed us. Joseph, in the Old Testament, is a great example of this, and we can learn much from how well he demonstrated stewardship in his life.

Sometimes we are discouraged because our needs are not met. One of the reasons for this could be because we have not yet taken them before God. At the end of James 4:2 it says, *'You do not have, because you do not ask God.'* Sometimes, we are so busy telling everyone else our needs that we neglect to tell the One who has the power to meet them.

Philippians 4:19 says, 'And my God will meet all your needs according to the riches of His glory in Christ Jesus.' Everything we have is given to us by God. Whatever we have, we did not earn ourselves, but it was by God's grace that it has been given to us.

When we don't have open hands to others and to God, we have a problem. Does God have to pry open our hands to get access to what we are holding on tightly to, or is He able to take anything He wants from our hand and use it for His glory?

Remember, if we have closed hands towards God, not only can He not use the things in our hands, but He can't put anything into our hands either.

What is it you desire God to do in you and through you? Have you asked Him? Or do you doubt that anything will change?

Matthew 4:4 and Deuteronomy 8:3 say that not only do we need food to strengthen our bodies, but we also need to feed on the Word of God so that we might be spiritually fed. We can be physically well fed but spiritually malnourished. We need to make sure we feed ourselves spiritually (see Jeremiah 15:16 and Job 23:12).

Our 'bread' comes from God – He is our source. It is our *daily* bread – not weekly, monthly or yearly. We need to rely on God daily for our needs – communing and having fellowship with Him regularly.

In our close relationships on earth there is a level of intimacy which takes time to develop. How much more do we need to invest time with our heavenly Father that we might have a deeper relationship with Him?

God tested the Israelites in the wilderness to trust Him for their manna each day. How well do you think we would do in the same situation? Would we rely on our own strength and try and save some manna for the next day like some of the Israelites tried to do, or would we have expectant hearts toward God in providing for us anew each day?

It all comes down to knowing who God is and therefore realising that we can put our complete trust in Him.

The question of the day is how well do we know God?

*Pam Wunderli*
*MAF Uganda*

# This Little Light of Mine...

*'John was a lamp that burned and gave light, and you chose for a time to enjoy his light.'*

(John 5:35)

John was a man who was sent from God with a specific mission – to prepare the way for the Messiah. He was in the mould of the Old Testament prophets and his ministry attracted a great following, even though it was fiery and focused on repentance. But John never lost sight of the fact that he was not the Christ. He was happy to point away from himself to Jesus: *'Behold the Lamb of God who takes away the sin of the world'* (John 1:29, 36).

Success didn't go to his head, and when the time came for some of his disciples to leave him and attach themselves to his cousin, he accepted it with good grace: *'He must become greater; I must become less'* (John 3:30).

Every follower of Jesus is called to be a witness, and like John to shine brightly in the world. There is, however, a cost to shining. The kind of light that Jesus refers to here is either a candle or, more likely, an oil lamp. Either way, the light only shines because something burns and is consumed in the process.

It reminds us that if we are to have a good testimony we will have to die to self, particularly to selfish ambition or the desire to be noticed, in order to point away from ourselves to Jesus. Our aim is not to draw attention to ourselves, but to help people to see Jesus.

As a young preacher I gave one of my first talks in a local Methodist chapel. In the pulpit, positioned to catch the eye of the preacher, was a small brass plaque with these words: 'Sir, We Would See Jesus'. In 40 years of preaching, I have never forgotten that golden rule.

Christian ministry, in whatever way it is expressed, is about giving glory to God. Christian witness, however it is demonstrated, puts the attention on Jesus and lets people know how wonderful He is. Wherever He has placed us, our calling is to be like John, a lamp that shines brightly.

**Reflection:**

> 'Don't light a lamp and hide it away; put it on a stand so it gives light all around.'
>
> (Matthew 5:15)

*Tony Horsfall*
*Pastoral Care Advisor*

# Lifting the Arms of Moses
(Exodus 17:8-13)

**M**oses knew the power of praise and the power of prayer. He acknowledged that the Lord was the One who sustained the Israelites and gave them victory over their enemies. Moses said, 'Tomorrow, I will stand at the top of the hill, with the rod of God in my hand.'

He knew what to do and he found that he needed to keep an attitude of praise and prayer for the army to win the battle.

When we read Exodus 17:8-13, we clearly see that it was the Lord who overcame, and that whenever Moses lowered his arms the Amalekites prevailed.

The Lord told Moses to write everything down for a memorial (verse 14). This was to remind them, and us, not to become proud in our own achievements. And so it was that, when Moses raised his hands to God, the Israelite army prevailed against their enemy.

This must have been very uncomfortable for Moses. Imagine having to hold your hands up for hours on end! Sometimes we find ourselves in uncomfortable situations – sometimes needing to stay there for a while. Verse 12 says 'until the sun went down' – so Moses spent all day with his arms lifted to the Lord!

We read that Moses' arms eventually became tired, which is hardly surprising! So his friends Aaron and Hur helped, assisted and supported him – holding up Moses' arms for him. In doing so, they helped the whole army.

They didn't say 'we will take over now', nor did they move him, but they brought a rock for Moses to sit on – which took further effort!

As Moses' friends had their part to do, so did those on the battlefield who were doing the fighting. But everyone realised that whatever they were doing, they needed the power of God to overcome the enemy. They needed people to pray to God and praise Him in order to persevere. The physical task had to be done, just as the spiritual battle needed to be fought.

Like Aaron and Hur, we need to support our leaders and those working for the Lord. We need to persevere in prayer.

1 Timothy 2:8 says, *'I desire that men should lift up holy hands in prayer without wrath'* (ie in agreement).

As Moses' friends held up his arms for him, may we come alongside others when they are weary. May we praise the Lord with them, pray for them and uphold them before the Lord, acknowledging the greatness of our God and remembering that we all need His power in our lives to overcome the enemy.

*Ruth Whitaker*
*Chief Executive, MAF UK*

# God's Always Got More

*'Look around from where you are.'*

(Genesis 13:14)

God sometimes says to us, 'You remember what has happened in the past, you know where you are now – but look around, because I want to show you all I have for you in the future!'

That's what God was saying to Abram, when he had just come out of Egypt and returned to the Promised Land. He had gone to Egypt because of famine in the Promised Land. But while in Egypt, Abram showed his lack of faith in God by deceiving Pharaoh, the ruler of Egypt.

Nevertheless, in spite of this, the Lord blessed him. We read in Genesis 13 that God had greatly increased Abram's riches and wealth.

I'm amazed how God sometimes blesses me – even when I am not walking fully in His will. He's a generous, loving God, always desiring to bless His children, whether they deserve it or not.

But Abram's deceit was discovered by Pharaoh and he was 'kicked out' of Egypt!

What did Abram do? He went back to the Promised Land and to Bethel, where he'd first met and acknowledged God. Genesis 13:4 says, *'There Abram called on the name of the Lord.'*

Whenever I haven't got things right I need to go back to God, seek Him, call upon Him and seek His will. I may need to do this regularly. In any case – it's a very good exercise.

God said to Abram, *'Lift up your eyes and look – look around from where you are!'* We need to do this not only when things have gone wrong, but also at different stages of life, and seek God's leading for the future. We need to stop, seek the Lord and 'look around'. God had a much bigger vision for Abram. He wanted him to see all the future promises He had for him.

Does God say that to me today? At what stage am I? Am I open to what He may have in the future? So often Scripture encourages us to look beyond where we are currently, and look with expectation to all that may yet be before us in God's plans, *e.g.* Isaiah 33:17, Joshua 13:1, Jeremiah 33:3, Philippians 3:13.

Has God given me past blessings, often undeserved? I need to remember He also wants to continue to bless and lead me. What does He still have ahead for me?

*Stuart King*
*Co-founder and President Emeritus, MAF International*

# Wisdom is The Principal Thing

*'Wisdom is the principal thing; therefore get wisdom.*
*And in all your getting, get understanding.*
*Let your heart retain my words;*
*Keep my commands, and live.*
*Get wisdom! Get understanding!*
*Do not forget, nor turn away from the words of my mouth.*
*Do not forsake her, and she will preserve you;*
*Love her, and she will keep you.*
*Wisdom is the principal thing;*
*Therefore get wisdom.*
*And in all your getting, get understanding.*
*Exalt her, and she will promote you;*
*She will bring you honour, when you embrace her.*
*She will place on your head an ornament of grace;*
*A crown of glory she will deliver to you.*

*Wisdom is the principal thing; therefore get wisdom.*
*And in all your getting, get understanding.*

*Happy is the man who finds wisdom,*
*And the man who gains understanding;*
*For her proceeds are better than the profits of silver,*
*And her gain than fine gold.*
*She is more precious than rubies,*
*And all the things you may desire cannot compare with her.*
*Length of days is in her right hand,*
*In her left hand riches and honour.*
*Her ways are ways of pleasantness,*
*And all her paths are peace.*

*Wisdom is the principal thing; therefore get wisdom.*
*And in all your getting, get understanding.*

*The Lord by wisdom founded the earth;*
*By understanding He established the heavens.*
*The fear of the Lord is the beginning of knowledge,*
*But fools despise wisdom and instruction.*

*My son, if you receive my words,*
*And treasure my commands within you,*
*So that you incline your ear to wisdom,*
*And apply your heart to understanding;*
*Yes, if you cry out for discernment,*
*And lift up your voice for understanding,*
*If you seek her as silver,*
*And search for her as for hidden treasures;*
*Then you will understand the fear of the Lord,*
*And find the knowledge of God.*
*For the Lord gives wisdom.*

*Wisdom is the principal thing; therefore let us get wisdom.'*

*'If anyone lacks wisdom, let him ask of God, who gives to all liberally and without reproach, and it will be given to him.*

*How beautiful wisdom is; for it comes from above and is therefore pure, full of quiet gentleness, peace loving and courteous; it allows discussion and is willing to yield to others. It is full of mercy and good deeds, wholehearted, straightforward and sincere.'*

(From Proverbs and James)